A Kids' Guide to
Hunger & Homelessness

How to Take Action!

Cathryn Berger Kaye, M.A.

free spirit
PUBLISHING®

Library of Congress Cataloging-in-Publication Data
Kaye, Cathryn Berger.
    A kids' guide to hunger and homelessness : how to take action / Cathryn Berger Kaye.
        p. cm.
    ISBN-13: 978-1-57542-240-4
    ISBN-10: 1-57542-240-9
  1. Homelessness—Juvenile literature. 2. Hunger—Juvenile literature. 3. Social action—Juvenile literature. 4. Service learning—Juvenile literature. 5. Young volunteers in social service—Juvenile literature. I. Title.
    HV4493.K39 2007
    362.5'574—dc22
2006038933

Service learning occurs in each of the fifty United States and internationally. Some project descriptions are attributed to specific schools or youth groups and identified by city, state, or region. All efforts have been made to ensure correct attribution. The names of the young people quoted throughout the book have been changed to protect their privacy.

The "Gotta Feed 'Em All" logo on page 13 is reprinted with permission of the City of West Hollywood.

The peanut sheller drawing on page 21 is reprinted with permission of Roey Rosenblith, Director of Outreach, Full Belly Project.

The excerpt and cover image on pages 24–25 are from *Soul Moon Soup* by Lindsay Lee Johnson (Front Street, an imprint of Boyds Mills Press, 2002). Reprinted with permission of Boyds Mills Press, Inc. Copyright © 2002 by Lindsay Lee Johnson.

Reading Level Grades 5–6; Interest Level Ages 10 & Up; Fountas & Pinnell Guided Reading Level W

Edited by Rebecca Aldridge and Meg Bratsch
Interior design by Jayne Curtis
Cover design by Marieka Heinlen

10 9 8 7 6 5 4
Printed in the United States of America
S18861210

Free Spirit Publishing Inc.
217 Fifth Avenue North, Suite 200
Minneapolis, MN 55401-1299
(612) 338-2068
help4kids@freespirit.com
www.freespirit.com

Free Spirit Publishing is a member of the Green Press Initiative, and we're committed to printing our books on recycled paper containing a minimum of 30% post-consumer waste (PCW). For every ton of books printed on 30% PCW recycled paper, we save 5.1 trees, 2,100 gallons of water, 114 gallons of oil, 18 pounds of air pollution, 1,230 kilo-watt hours of energy, and .9 cubic yards of landfill space. At Free Spirit it's our goal to nurture not only young people, but nature too!

Printed on recycled paper
including 50%
post-consumer waste

Acknowledgments

As always, the "village" concept comes into play with any service learning publication. To the many service learning colleagues who share stories and examples—thank you! To the youth who demonstrate dedication and passion—your ideas and vision inspire us all. To all at Free Spirit Publishing who contribute in myriad ways to the service learning field—hooray! And to my family who provides unconditional support and love—my heart is most grateful.

What's Inside

What Kids Think
of Working to End Hunger & Homelessness

"I learned what it means to be a contributing member in a community. Having the privilege to learn about the homeless community was a very great and heartwarming experience." —Justin, age 14

"People are all the same despite their living status. We should never stereotype people." —Skye, age 14

"This project opened my eyes to all the different ways that a person can become impoverished, and also how hard it is to get out of poverty. . . . Many of the homeless people I talked to told me to go to college. They were living proof that not going to college really narrows the job opportunities. Now I feel more inspired to go to college."
—Tyla, age 16

"I learned that there is a lot more to homelessness than the people you see on the street. I learned that we can do a lot to help." —Max, age 12

"I feel more open to people after this service learning project. By understanding what impoverished people in our community have to go through, I can learn how to help them." —Lindsay, age 15

"I learned that even though I might not have solved world hunger, or ended global wars, I made a couple of ladies very happy, and if everyone could do that in this world, the world would be a better place." —MJ, age 13

"I learned that I really need to work on my social skills, as far as overcoming being judgmental and shy. I learned that homeless people are just like everyone else." —Amanda, age 14

"I used to say I wanted to make a difference in people's lives when I grow up. Doing our project made me realize that I can make a difference right now." —Serena, age 14

What Do You Know?

How many people in the world do you think go to bed hungry every night?

☐ 100,000   ☐ 5,000,000   ☐ 800,000,000

What do you think are the major reasons people become homeless today? Check all that you think are important.

☐ Unemployment   ☐ Low wages

☐ Natural disasters   ☐ Family problems

☐ Rising housing costs   ☐ Illness

☐ Too many people

How many people in the world do you think live on less than $2 a day?

☐ 15% of the global population—about 900 million people

☐ 25% of the global population—about 1.5 billion people

☐ 50% of the global population—about 3 billion people

What do these questions about hunger and homelessness have to do with you? *Everything.* These issues affect people in your world every day, including people in your community and maybe even in your neighborhood or in your school. What do hunger and homelessness mean? How can you become involved in helping others? That's what this book is about: ways to use what you learn to make a meaningful contribution to your world. To serve through service learning.

"Every individual matters. Every individual has a role to play. Every individual makes a difference. And we have a choice: What sort of difference do we want to make?"

—Jane Goodall, biologist

Starting Now

Probably everyone wants to put an end to hunger and homelessness. However you found this book or it found you, these activities will help you discover a way to address the problem. How? By learning how to **prepare**, turn ideas into **action**, **reflect** on what you do, and **demonstrate** how you did it. Whatever you choose to do, whether it's helping an organization or starting a project on your own, the time to start is now.

Did You Get the Right Answers?

Here are the answers to the questions on page 2: 800 million people—men, women, and children—go to bed hungry every night. All of the reasons listed contribute to why people around the globe are homeless. And half the world's population lives on less than $2 a day.

These questions had "right" answers. Many activities in this book include questions designed to get you thinking, learning, sharing ideas, and even coming up with more questions. In these cases, few have "right" answers. Rather, they are simply opportunities to learn, experience, and get involved.

A Note About Using This Book

This guide is written for use by classes or youth groups, so the activity directions assume you are in a group of around 15 to 30 students. However, smaller groups, families, and individuals can easily adapt every activity. If you are using the book on your own, consider finding a friend to participate with you.

Tips for Using This Book

You are holding a written guide, but you will find other guides around you—adults you meet who are involved in service learning, friends and other students working with you, and community members who are eager to help.

★ Keep track of your thoughts and observations in this book. Write in it whenever and wherever you want!

★ You might also want to start your own service learning journal in a notebook.

★ Share your ideas with others, no matter how far-fetched they may seem!

★ Let your creativity inspire you.

Service + Learning = Service Learning

Service:
Service means contributing or helping to benefit others and the common good.

Learning:
Learning means gaining understanding of a subject or skill through study, instruction, or experience.

Service Learning:
The ideas of service and learning combine to create service learning. **Preparation, action, reflection,** and **demonstration** are the four stages of service learning. By understanding how these stages work, you can make plans more effectively to help in your community.

Stage 1: Preparation

Imagine that you decide to throw a birthday party for kids who live at a homeless shelter. What would you do

> "I cannot predict the wind but I can have my sail ready."
> —E. F. Schumacher, author

first? **Prepare.** You already have experience preparing for many activities, whether getting ingredients for baking brownies or warming up for a basketball game. Make a list of three ways you would get ready to throw this birthday party.

Birthday Party Preparation

1. ....

2. ....

3. ....

Now look at the following list. Did you have similar ideas?

- Visit the shelter.
- Learn about homelessness in the community.
- Talk to the director of the shelter.
- Talk to the kids at the shelter to find out their interests.
- Organize a collection of birthday presents and party supplies.

Stage 2: Action

Once you are prepared with the background knowledge you need, you can create and carry out your **action** plan. Most often, you will take action in one or more of the following four ways.

Direct Service:
Your service involves face-to-face interactions with people, or close contact with them.

Indirect Service:
Your action is not seen by the people who may benefit from it, but it meets a real need.

Advocacy:
What you do makes others aware of an issue and encourages them to take action to change a situation.

Research:
You gather and report on information that helps a community.

Which of these ways best describes the example of throwing a birthday party for kids at a shelter? What if you wanted to take action to reduce hunger and homelessness using each of these ways? With a partner, come up with an example for each and write them below. Keep in mind that in all types of service learning, everyone is meant to benefit and learn from each other.

Taking Action Against Hunger & Homelessness

Direct Service:

Indirect Service:

Advocacy:

Research:

Stage 3: Reflection

What is one piece of information you have learned so far that you want to remember?

....

What is one idea you now have that you didn't have before you opened this book?

....

When you answer these questions, you are participating in **reflection**: looking at your experience to determine what it has to do with you. Reflection takes place all along the way: as you prepare, as you do the service, and as you demonstrate what you have learned and accomplished. You will find reflection built into many of the activities in this book. When you see the Time for Reflection symbol, follow the directions to special reflection pages.

Stage 4: Demonstration

Demonstration is the stage where you take the opportunity to let others know what you have learned and what good community work you have done. Are you an artist? Do you like to perform? Do you enjoy writing? Do you like taking photos? Are you a computer whiz? You could use any of these skills or talents to demonstrate your service learning. Circle ways you might want to **demonstrate** what you accomplish:

Make a mural.

Create a Web site.

Build a display for a local library.

Write an article for your school or community newspaper.

Put together a video or audio recording.

Perform a skit for another class or youth group.

Create a brochure showing the steps you followed.

What Is Missing?

A school has an annual food drive. Every day for a week, students hear an announcement asking everyone to bring in cans of food and put them in the box by the office. Someone in the office delivers the boxes to an agency after volunteers spend time removing cans without labels or ones that are too old to donate. Many of the food items are not what is needed. What is missing from this service plan? With a partner, describe what a food drive would look like that includes:

PREPARATION:

ACTION:

REFLECTION:

DEMONSTRATION:

Competition as Service?

In some schools, the class that brings in the most cans for the food drive wins a prize, like a pizza party. This can lead students to care more about winning than helping. How could kids in a school *collaborate*—work together—rather than compete, to hold the best food drive ever? Add ideas for *collaboration* to the food drive plan you and your partner developed.

Learning About Hunger & Homelessness

What Does It Mean to Be Hungry?

How would both your body and mind feel if you couldn't eat breakfast and lunch?

If you had little or no food for many days in a row, what would happen to you?

People often say, "I'm hungry!" But is hunger a growling stomach before lunch, a craving for an after-school snack, or something more? In school you learn about nutrition and how eating a balanced diet builds strong bodies, helps you think clearly, and provides the energy you need to live your life. When people do not have enough nutritious food to eat on a daily basis, this is real hunger. Hunger that continues over weeks and months is called *chronic hunger*. People who experience chronic hunger may get sick more often, and their ability to study or work may be affected.

What Does It Mean to Be Homeless?

Home may be a small word, but it is a big idea. It is more than shelter, more than a place to eat and sleep. It often includes people and a feeling of safety. On television news you probably have seen how easily "home" can be swept away by a tsunami or hurricane, or destroyed by a fire. What goes through your head when you see someone living in a car or out of a shopping cart? What might it feel like to be without a house *and* without food every day? Take a moment to consider: **What does home mean to you?** On a separate sheet of paper, make a list, paragraph, poem, song, or short story, or create a drawing, painting, or collage to express your ideas.

Ending Hunger & Homelessness

It's probably obvious to you that we need to end hunger and homelessness. Every action that you take helps, and so does the work of community members, businesses, and governments. Whether you make plans alone or work with these groups, you help address the true causes of hunger and homelessness, so that some day, every person in the world will have a safe place to live and enough nutritious food to eat.

Meet Kids in Action: Part 1

Every day kids improve their communities and our world. The stories in the "Meet Kids in Action" chapters of this book tell of kids who learn about and provide service to people experiencing hunger and homelessness.

Ready to Help in Tajikistan

In Tajikistan in central Asia, students in grades 8 through 11 have joined Youth Leadership Clubs to improve society through volunteer work and community service. Every month, the students get ideas from kids in different parts of Tajikistan and then create a plan for young leaders to work on. One of these plans resulted in Ready to Help, a project to feed students in orphanages. On Global Youth Service Day, the youth leaders joined with students from the Future Leaders Exchange Program (sponsored by the U.S. government) and other volunteers to serve meals for disabled and homeless children in orphanages. While the food was cooking, the volunteers played games and made art with the children. According to the participants, "This type of service activity really brightens each and every orphan's life, letting them know that they aren't alone in this world."

> To learn about grants for National and Global Youth Service Day, visit Youth Service America at www.ysa.org.

Recycling for Others

Eighth-grade Punahou School students in Honolulu, Hawaii, wanted to purchase holiday gifts for families in a homeless shelter. To raise the needed funds, they decided to sell earth-friendly products they made from recycled materials. A new project was born: Project CHEERRR (Creatively Helping Educate Everyone to Reduce, Reuse, and Recycle). In science classes, students accepted the challenge of turning people's trash into treasures. Students in math classes determined the amount of supplies needed and set fair prices for the products created. And in social studies classes, they focused on advertising and marketing the products. The result? Students made juice box purses and pieces of jewelry created from wire, glass, and even bottle caps, and they sold their creations for a total of $800. Then, they went shopping for the parents and children at the shelter. When delivering the gifts, the students realized their project had been about more than classroom lessons—it was about life.

> As you read these stories, do any ideas come to mind? Write them down as you read. Use them to start discussions and to help you take action.

Defining What You Know

Dictionaries provide one kind of definition. But definitions written in your own words can be more memorable because they are tied to what you have seen, heard, or experienced. As you gain life experience, your definitions may change.

Cover the right-hand column below. On the left-hand side are important terms to know and, more important, to know what they mean to you. After you complete the left column, compare your ideas to what is on the right.

Choosing Your Words
In this book you will find the phrases "people experiencing homelessness" or "people who are homeless" instead of "homeless people." This word choice is intentional. It helps us remember the humanity of people first, before describing their circumstance.

Hunger: What it means to me:

List two things besides food that a person could feel hungry for.

1. ....

2. ....

Homelessness: What it means to me:

List two different kinds of homes people live in around the globe.

1. ....

2. ....

Poverty: What it means to me:

What do you imagine a person in poverty would want most of all?

Hunger: The lack of good food needed to keep people healthy. The term can also describe other wants or needs, such as a desire, or hunger, for knowledge or love.

Homelessness: Not having a permanent or long-term place to live. Most of the world's people live in permanent homes, like houses or huts. However, in nomadic cultures where moving from place to place is a natural part of life, home is considered to be where you are at a certain time. In general, having safe shelter is a basic need for survival, especially for children.

Poverty: Not having a way to satisfy basic material needs (like food or clothes) and comforts (like beds and blankets).

What Causes Hunger & Homelessness?

As a baby, you learned about hunger. You cried when you needed food. And people gave you what you needed. Now you're able to help yourself. You might be among the lucky people who have always had a roof over their heads and enough food to eat.

But in this complex world, many people cannot provide these basic needs for themselves and their families and require assistance from others. People who experience hunger and homelessness are found in every country and in most every community, whether country, city, or suburb.

In southern Africa, 38 million people are currently starving because AIDS, war, poverty, poor governance, and climate changes make recovery from the famine there nearly impossible.

The causes of hunger and homelessness are many. People throughout history have been uprooted and made homeless because of war, drought (not enough water for crops), or famine (not enough food). In many countries, new settlers or governments drove native populations—such as American Indians in the United States—from their homes. Today, people may face homelessness after losing jobs, because of unexpected medical expenses, or due to a rise in housing costs. Some people may not be able to get jobs because of discrimination based on their race, gender, or social class. Natural disasters, such as floods, tornados, hurricanes, earthquakes, and fires, can devastate a community or destroy crops, so there is less food to eat. Some people who want to grow crops may not have the land, seeds, or tools they need. In some cases, hunger is made worse by people not being educated about good nutrition.

A long civil war in Colombia, South America, has displaced 2.5 million people from their homes.

You spend a lot of time in school. In many parts of the world, there are no schools for kids to attend. How is having a good education part of solving hunger and homelessness? Write your ideas here:

Do some people or groups help cause hunger and homelessness in the world? Do some help solve these issues instead? Maybe some do both. Decide how the people and groups below can be part of the cause and/or part of the solution to hunger and homelessness.

	How They're Part of the Cause	How They're Part of the Solution
Kids		
Parents		
Businesses		
Governments		

Meet Kids in Action: Part 2

Gotta Feed 'Em All

After stocking food at a local food bank, middle and high school students in West Hollywood, California, learned that the food supply runs low during summer. One student had an idea: "Let's hold a food drive in the spring!" The students worked with city government, schools, and food bank partners to create the "Gotta Feed 'Em All" food campaign. Every April, their student-designed logo (at right) appears on street banners around the city, and collection containers are placed in markets, schools, and city hall. The food bank welcomes these contributions that address a real community need.

"I learned how much work it takes to run a food shelf. The way people go through food there is amazing. I never knew how much food it takes to feed one person. Hunger is a real issue in our world and we need to do something to stop it from growing."
—Corey, 13, West Hollywood, California

Harvesting to Help

How does our garden grow? An eighth-grade science class from Chariho Middle School teamed with fourth graders at Richmond Elementary in Richmond, Rhode Island, to plant a garden in an unused greenhouse on school grounds. They read books and did research to find out what grows best in a heated greenhouse during winter. To decide where to donate food from their garden, students learned about hunger and homelessness and visited nearby service agencies. One student summed up the results: "My thinking about homelessness has changed . . . because at first I did not care about the people who are homeless. But after going to the shelter and seeing the people who live in it, I figured that homelessness is a pretty big issue in Rhode Island, and it should be taken seriously or the number of people who are homeless could grow."

··· TIME FOR ⌖ REFLECTION ⊒

Turn to pages 37–38, and choose a reflection activity to complete.

Getting the Facts:
Who Is Hungry? Who Is Homeless?

Think about each of the following populations, and brainstorm why this population might be hungry or homeless. If you're in a large group, form small groups so each group can think about one of the populations listed.

Immigrants   Children

Seniors   ?   Veterans

Families   Unemployed

Read about these populations below and on the following pages. Then, imagine someone who works at a local service agency (food or clothing bank, homeless shelter, etc.) will be visiting your class or group. Prepare a question to ask this person about each of these populations.

Immigrants: Many immigrants leave their countries because of poverty or mistreatment and the desire to have a better life. They may arrive in a new country with little more than the clothes they are wearing. Finding affordable homes and jobs can be difficult. Learning a new language and adapting to a new lifestyle can add more hardship.

FACT: In Texas, 8 percent of immigrant households experience severe hunger. This percentage is ten times higher than the rest of the U.S. population.

Your Question:..

....

Families: All parents desire the best for their children. However, families that don't earn enough money can experience food shortage or loss of their homes. Learning how to create a budget and manage money has helped some people at risk for hunger or homelessness.

FACT: In the United States, 13.8 million children live in households that are poor and need help providing food for every family member. Many of these poor households have at least one working parent. Even with one parent working, it can be hard to feed a family.

Your Question:..
....

Children: Whether a young child lives in a family or alone on the streets, too many children go hungry every day or have poor nutrition.

FACT: In Canada, approximately 41 percent of the people getting assistance through food banks are children. In the United States, one in five people in a soup kitchen line is a child, with nearly 14 million American children facing hunger. Globally, more than 16,000 children die from hunger-related causes every day. That's one child every five seconds.

Your Question:..
....

Veterans: Veterans are people who have served in the armed forces, usually during a time of war. In the United States, many end up homeless due to the high cost of housing, lack of health care, difficulty finding employment, and physical or mental problems linked to their military service.

FACT: On any single day in the United States, more than 200,000 veterans will sleep on the streets or in shelters. More than twice that many experience homelessness sometime during a year.

Your Question:..
....

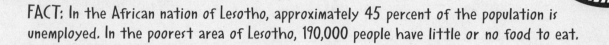

Unemployed: Around the world, unemployment is a leading cause of hunger and homelessness.

FACT: In the African nation of Lesotho, approximately 45 percent of the population is unemployed. In the poorest area of Lesotho, 190,000 people have little or no food to eat.

Your Question: ....

....

Seniors: Housing and health care costs rise, but many senior citizens live on an income that doesn't change, so they may live at or below poverty level. Some elderly people even have to choose between paying for food and housing or buying life-saving medicine.

FACT: More than 4 million Americans over age 65 are dependent on Second Harvest, an independent organization for food relief. This number doesn't include many other elderly Americans who receive food assistance from the government or other organizations.

Your Question: ....

....

An estimated 1 billion people in the world lack adequate housing, including 100 million who are completely homeless. Nearly 10 million people in South Africa live in slums and poor housing. In Japan, an estimated 24,000 people are homeless. In the United States, more than 800,000 people are without homes on any given night, and only 250,000 spaces are available in shelters.

... TIME FOR REFLECTION

Turn to pages 37–38, and choose a reflection activity to complete.

Looking Back:
Historical Moments & Actions

In school you may have learned about times in history when people lived in poverty and were homeless or hungry. Think of two historical events in which people experienced hunger or homelessness.

When in history?	Who was affected?	What happened?

A Response to Hunger

Imagine that famine has hit a country where most people live on potatoes. Now the potato plants are dying from a mysterious fungus. Food is hard to find and people are dying. How can one person help? What good can a group of people do?

Between 1845 and 1849, approximately 1.5 million people died during the Irish potato famine, over a third of Ireland's population at that time. How do actions taken long ago have an impact today? Read the following stories to find out.

Alexis Soyer

Alexis Soyer was a chef in the mid-1830s at an expensive London restaurant. Soyer was very successful in this job, but his observation of poverty on the city's streets led him to use his cooking talents to help those in need. Soyer began teaching women how to feed the hungry poor. When many of the people in Ireland began dying because of the potato famine, the Irish government invited Soyer to set up a soup kitchen in Dublin that could serve 5,000 meals a day. Soyer did that and more. He placed a huge pot over a fire, set the whole thing on wheels, and rolled hot soup through Dublin's streets. His method successfully fed 9,000 people a day. Years later he wrote a cookbook, *Soyer's Shilling Cookery for the People*, teaching people how to make inexpensive meals. Over 110,000 copies were sold in four months.

> We learn that the Government have resolved forthwith to despatch M. Soyer, the chef de cuisine of the Reform Club, to Ireland, with ample instructions to provide his soups for the starving millions of Irish people. . .
> —The Cork Examiner, February 26, 1847

To learn more about Alexis Soyer, read *The Adventurous Chef: Alexis Soyer* by Ann Arnold (Francis Foster Books/Farrar Straus Giroux, 2002).

YOUR TURN

Who in your neighborhood goes out of their way to help improve the lives of others? By asking people you know or by reading newspapers, identify at least one of your neighbors who helps with hunger or homelessness. You might choose to interview this person during your own service learning experience.

The Choctaw Contribution

Can one helpful act inspire more acts? In the United States in 1847, just 16 years after being forced to move off their sacred land in the historic event known as the Trail of Tears, the Choctaw Indians collected $170 (worth $5,000 today) for the starving Irish people across the ocean. Other tribes joined in and together they sent $710 (worth over $20,000 today) in famine relief to Ireland.

We have walked the trail of tears. The Irish people walk it now. We can help them as we could not help ourselves. Our help will be like an arrow shot through time. It will land many winters from now to wait as a blessing for our unborn generations.

From *The Long March: The Choctaw's Gift to Irish Famine Relief*

In 1992, nearly 150 years after the Great Potato Famine in Ireland, famine in the African country of Somalia became international news. To honor the long-ago Choctaw contribution and raise money for Somalia, eight Irish people walked 500 miles of the Choctaw Trail of Tears. By walking in the footsteps of people who, despite their own problems, responded to the needs of others, these eight people raised funds for the hungry and raised awareness about the connection between people of all nations.

> To learn more about the Choctaw contribution, read *The Long March: The Choctaw Gift to Irish Famine Relief* by Marie-Louise Fitzpatrick (Tricycle Press, 2001).

YOUR TURN

What is your reaction to what the eight Irish people did? After reading these stories, do you think one person can make a difference? How would you like to honor what other people have experienced?

When Disaster Strikes

On December 26, 2004, an earthquake shook the floor of the Indian Ocean, setting off tsunamis—giant waves that move at tremendous speeds. These walls of water destroyed everything in their paths—homes, businesses, hotels, and most important, all forms of life. Over 200,000 people died in Indonesia, Sri Lanka, India, and Thailand.

In August 2005, the U.S. Gulf Coast region was hit by multiple hurricanes, causing major damage to Louisiana, Alabama, and Mississippi. In addition to the terrible loss of lives, more than 1.3 million had to leave their towns and cities to find safe shelter.

These natural disasters created an immediate need for rescue efforts, clean water and food, plus clothing and other items to keep people healthy and safe. In these events and other similar disasters, volunteers—people of all backgrounds from across the globe—were among the first to respond. Help may have been given on-site, such as rescuing people and moving debris, or long-distance, such as sending money and donating food. Kids joined the effort by collecting clothes, food, and school supplies, and by raising money in creative ways like making lemonade and popcorn stands. They continue helping.

During the summer of 2006, 48 young people ages 12 to 25 involved with the Dakshina Lanka Buddhist Association worked for four months to build 50 houses in Sri Lanka for people left homeless by the tsunami tragedy. In addition to getting a crash course in construction, the students also gained leadership and organizational skills.

Also during the summer of 2006, 481 students in fifth through eighth grade in Mississippi, Louisiana, and Texas participated in the Gulf Coast WalkAbout. Each class investigated community needs and resources. Based on their observations and information gathered, students designed service projects that included the following:

New Orleans students built three new bus benches to place near their school where previous benches had been destroyed by the hurricanes.

In Mississippi, students placed birdhouses in the wild to house birds whose habitats were destroyed by the hurricanes.

In Texas, where many families settled after Hurricane Katrina, students filled emergency preparation bags with personal supplies to donate in their community.

To learn about the impact of the tsunami in Thailand, read *Tsunami: Helping Each Other* by Ann Morris and Heidi Larson (Millbrook Press, 2005).

To learn more about the WalkAbout program, visit the National Youth Leadership Council Web site at www.nylc.org.

YOUR TURN

Every community is at risk for some kind of natural disaster. What preparation is needed in your community? How can students help people who are poor or homeless be prepared? Write your ideas here:

Making History: The Full Belly Project

The previous section gave you a glimpse of what happened in the past. Here's a story about what is happening now and creative ways people are making a difference.

Meet Roey Rosenblith, who began participating in service learning projects as a middle school student. As part of his service, he had the opportunity to visit Peru. He didn't expect it to be a life-changing event, but it was!

Roey was instructed to bring small toys to give to children in remote villages during his trip. Roey says, "I handed a ball to a boy and took his photo. Back home, the photo showed a malnourished child holding a ball. It made no sense. I was from a developed country with endless resources and I gave him a ball. This seemed worthless. Too often wealthy countries export items to developing nations that don't really give people what they need to make their lives better."

Several years later, as a college student, Roey heard about a person named Jock Brandis and the portable peanut sheller he had developed. A half billion people on the planet depend on peanuts as their main source of protein. Women in Africa spend 4 billion hours every year shelling peanuts by hand. This work is very hard and takes a lot of time; children even miss school to shell peanuts during the harvest. Brandis created a machine to improve this situation. In 2003, he and a group of others began the Full Belly Project, which offers the machine's design technology for free to poor countries. Roey says, "Next thing I knew, I had made a commitment to help the Full Belly Project." Now a college graduate, Roey remains dedicated to the project.

"As a teen, I began to realize that problems facing people in developing countries are our problems. In today's world, an idea can start in one place and move fast. To be part of this process is fulfilling. Helping others have a full belly makes the work worthwhile."
—Roey Rosenblith

To learn more, visit www.fullbellyproject.org.

YOUR TURN

On your own or in a group, select one of the problems below. Design a product that would make a difference. On a sheet of paper, draw this product and describe three steps you would take to put it to work.

• Lack of clean drinking water in a polluted neighborhood or village
• People in need of dry clothing after a flood

Learning from Reading:
Soul Moon Soup

Books can help you learn about situations you've never experienced. In the chapter you're about to read from Lindsay Lee Johnson's *Soul Moon Soup*, you will meet Phoebe Rose, a girl living on city streets with her mother. They move into a shelter for families who are homeless and from there, Phoebe rides the bus to school.

If you are working in a large group, form groups of four to read and discuss "Secrets of the Shelter" on pages 24–25. Assign each person in the group one of the "connector" roles below. Each connector's job is to lead a group discussion about the story from a specific point of view. He or she asks the questions listed (along with others that come to mind) and encourages group members to respond. Choose one person to read the story aloud to the rest of the group. Feel free to write notes and ideas in the Literature Circle on the following page. If you are working alone, consider the questions under each connector and give your own answers.

Personal Connector:
Ask questions that connect the story to group members' experiences, such as:
1. Do any characters remind you of people you know? How?
2. Have you been in situations similar to what is described in the book? What happened?
3. How have you or people you know resolved similar situations?

Literary Connector:
Ask questions that connect this story to other stories group members have read, such as:
1. Which characters remind you of characters from other stories? Why?
2. What situations are similar to what happens in other stories?
3. What might Phoebe Rose say about these other characters or situations?

Service Connector:
Ask questions that connect this story to ideas for service projects, such as:
1. What needs to be fixed in this situation?
2. Did any characters in this story participate in service activities?
3. What service ideas did you think of when you read this story?

School Connector:
Ask questions that connect this story to your school, such as:
1. What were the school experiences of characters in this story?
2. What ideas in this story have you learned about or experienced in school?
3. What do you think people your age would learn by reading this story?

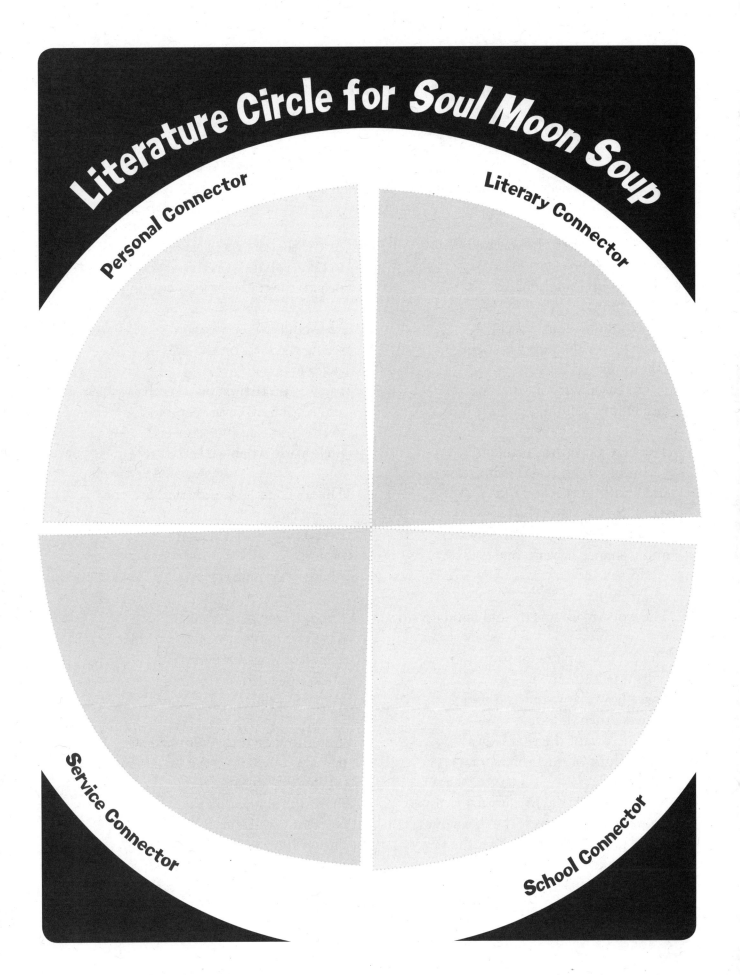

Literature Circle for *Soul Moon Soup*

Personal Connector

Literary Connector

Service Connector

School Connector

"Secrets of the Shelter" from *Soul Moon Soup*

In this prose poem, Phoebe Rose, age 11, describes life "in the hard poor middle of the city," where she sleeps with her mother in doorways and homeless shelters.

I especially hated the way we'd
start the day
rounded up for school on the
shelter bus.
All around the city it went,
stopping for the kids who slept
mat to mat
in the basements of churches
and empty buildings nobody wants.

The best places had blankets,
bathrooms with real flushing toilets,
sinks with mirrors on top.
At St. Steven's everybody got
a three-minute turn in the shower
and a chance to wash one load
of clothes.

The worst place was the old animal
testing lab.
Once it was a place for squirting
hairspray into rabbits' eyes
to see how many squirts it took
to make them blind.
Wouldn't want the ritzy ladies
getting hurt on their hairspray.

Now those torture rooms are places
for poor folks to sleep, the lucky ones.
Some people with money for the tickets
play to take a chance
on the money-winning lottery.

At the shelters we played for free
to take a chance on the
mat-on-the-cold-tile-floor-winning lottery.

I felt guilty when we won,
seeing the look on the eyes of
other mamas
packing up their snot-nosed babies
and setting off seventeen blocks
to the next slap in the face.
I felt worse when we lost.

There's good luck and bad luck, the
lottery lady said.
Everybody gets their share
of both.
That's what makes it fair.

I said, If one person's good luck
has to be another person's bad luck,
it spoils things for everybody.
Luck, I decided, is nothing
to depend on.

One thing even the winners never got:
privacy.
Shelter life was always
share and share alike.
Not just with other folks.
Shelter life was R and R,
a little rest and relaxation
with the roaches and the rats.

Then it was early up and out
for the special
poor-kids breakfast in the school
cafeteria.
All the cereal, bread, applesauce,
and milk
came wrapped or boxed in
little packages.
I don't remember ever
seeing Mama cook.

One time my locker partner gave me
a bottle of shampoo,
a pink bar of soap, and a washcloth
all tied up together pretty as
you please.
It's from my mother, I don't care,
she told me, backing off
when I threw the stuff away.

I slipped out of social studies early
to see if I could find that priceless
treasure in the trash,
but it was gone.
Now, who could I talk to
about a thing like that?
A sister, I guess,
if I had one.

Writing *Soul Moon Soup*—An Interview with Author Lindsay Lee Johnson

"When I began writing *Soul Moon Soup*, I did not think about 'homelessness.' I begin with a character who has a story to tell. She lived in my mind first, but her story is fed by my personal experience. As a volunteer at various shelters, I saw individuals in difficult circumstances, people experiencing homelessness rather than 'homeless people' as a group. Labels can stop us from wanting to get involved and take action. People having difficulties certainly don't choose their circumstances. In these pages I hope readers find the courage to connect with people around them who may need something they can give. *Soul Moon Soup* is the most meaningful story I have written. I hope Phoebe's voice is passed along. Then I will have accomplished something worthwhile."

TIME FOR REFLECTION 3

Turn to pages 37–38, and choose a reflection activity to complete.

Meet Kids in Action: Part 3

Understanding Poverty

At Einstein Middle School in Seattle, Washington, 120 eighth graders did more than read about poverty. In English classes, they read *Slake's Limbo*, a novel about a boy living on the streets. Students in math classes looked at the money side of poverty. And in science classes, they looked at how living situations affect health. Then, students led an Oxfam Hunger Banquet in which kids were placed in groups and fed different meals based on actual world hunger statistics. Guest speakers at the banquet talked about poverty in their community. With this background knowledge, students volunteered in downtown Seattle service agencies. They prepared and served food, gave pedicures, and collected food and other needed items to give away. After volunteering, students wrote reports, published zines, created digital videos, and organized and conducted an evening exhibition to teach others what they had learned.

To read a classic tale of one boy's survival on the streets of New York City, check out *Slake's Limbo* by Felice Holman (Aladdin; Reprint edition, 1986).

Oxfam Hunger Banquet

An Oxfam Hunger Banquet is a group dinner without much food. Each person is randomly assigned to a group based on world hunger statistics.

• **Fifteen percent** of the diners are placed in the high-income group; they sit at a table and enjoy a three-course meal.

• **Twenty-five percent** of the people attending are placed in the middle-income group; they sit in chairs and eat rice and beans.

• **Sixty percent** of the attendees sit on the floor and receive only rice and water. They represent the low-income group, and for one meal, they share the experience of the millions of people throughout the world who live in poverty.

To learn more, visit Oxfam America at www.oxfamamerica.org. For a hunger banquet computer experience, visit www.hungerbanquet.org.

A Call to Action

Following is an interview with Francis Moore Lappé, an author and well-known speaker. Her work helps people understand the causes of global hunger and poverty.

> "The outrage of hunger amidst plenty will never be solved by 'experts' somewhere. It will only be solved when people like you and me decide to act."
> —Francis Moore Lappé, author and activist

"No one wants another child to die of hunger but it happens every day by the thousands. Food 'experts' once claimed that population growth had exceeded the earth's limits to feed us. Today, we know this is false. We produce enough food to make each of us chubby.

> Infant and child mortality are viewed as a reliable measure of hunger. If mothers aren't eating properly, they have underweight babies who are more vulnerable to death in the first year.

"People go hungry not because of lack of food but because they don't have access to jobs and land to grow food. Exchanging goods and services has been around from early tribal days. In today's global market, only some people get wealthy while billions of people don't even have enough to eat. This is how we *create* hunger.

"People worry about hunger, global warming, and terrorism, but I see only one real crisis in today's world: our *feelings* of powerlessness to do something about our problems. Our voices can make the market work for everybody. One idea is creating a 'right to food.' In fact, 187 countries signed an agreement confirming this right. This idea becomes real when translated into action by regular citizens. By us.

"In Belo Horizonte, Brazil's fourth largest city, the Zero Hunger Campaign is in full gear reducing infant mortality by 50 percent. One practical idea: Farmers set up produce stands in the communities with affordable prices. In Bolivia, people are changing laws to increase land use for farms and schools, feeding the body and the mind. In Bangladesh, people who live in small villages are using a system called microcredit to provide loans based on group trust and developing businesses that improve their lives.

"What can you do? Use your voice, be a contributor, be a doer—and with service learning you can. You learn skills that make you powerful. You find your place in the community. You take risks, ask questions, get engaged. Along the way, you create friendships and connections. You are never bored! Life becomes an adventure. Find a buddy or two willing to act with you. It's not a 'you should,' it's a 'we can!' It's how we find our power to create the world we want, a world good for all of us!"

> To learn more about Frances Moore Lappé and the organization she founded with her daughter to help people around the globe, visit www.smallplanetinstitute.org.

Getting Started:
What Does Your Community Need?

The kids you've read about in this workbook based their projects on real community needs. Now it's your turn to find out the needs in your community so you can make a plan for action.

Use the questions in the following four categories as guides for learning more about hunger and homelessness in your area. If you're working in a large group, form four smaller groups, with each group focusing on one category and gathering information in a different way.

Media

What media (newspapers, TV stations, Web sites) in your community might have helpful information for you? List ways you can work with different media to learn about hunger and homelessness in your community.

Interviews

Think of a person who is knowledgeable about hunger and homelessness in your area—perhaps someone who works at a service agency, a government office, or a school, or someone who has been hungry or homeless. Write questions you would ask this person in an interview.

Surveys

A survey can help you find out what people know about hunger and homelessness and get ideas for helping. Who could you survey—students, family members, neighbors? How many surveys would you want to have completed? Write three survey questions.

Who to survey: How many surveys:

Questions for the survey:

1.

2.

3.

Observation and Experience

What ways are there to gather information through your own observation and experience? Where would you go? What would you do there? How would you keep track of what you find out?

Next Step: Share your ideas. Make a plan for gathering information in the four ways just discussed. If you are working in small groups, each group may want to involve people in other groups. For example, everyone could help conduct the survey and collect the results. Record the information you learn in the next chapter, "Our Community Needs."

Turn to pages 37–38, and choose a reflection activity to complete.

Our Community Needs
What I Learned From . . .

 Media:

 Interviews:

 Surveys:

 Observation and Experience:

As a result of your investigation, what do you think are the most important needs in your community involving hunger and homelessness?

Which method of gathering information did you like best? Why?

Who Is Helping?
Government & Community Groups

Who is helping with hunger and homelessness? Learning about who addresses these issues in the world can help you plan your service learning project, find partners to work with, and make your contribution count.

Government agencies and community organizations are two kinds of groups that help with hunger and homelessness. They work to meet immediate needs (like making sure people have safe places to sleep) and to find long-term solutions (like helping people get jobs to pay for housing). They are:

- local—in your city
- regional—in your state or province
- national—across your country
- international—across the globe (while no single government is "international," the United Nations organization is one way the governments of many nations work together on problems like hunger and homelessness)

Where to begin? To learn about government and community groups, contact social service departments or the office of an elected official in your area. You might also start with a local food bank or homeless shelter.

Research Tips

PHONE BOOK—the front pages often list local, state, and national government offices.

THE INTERNET—government offices and many community organizations have easy-to-use Web pages with information about issues and how to learn more.

SCHOOL OFFICE—ask if there are lists of community organizations your school works with already.

ELECTED OFFICIALS—they often have people on staff to answer questions and provide contact information and resources.

THIS WORKBOOK—visit the Web sites listed throughout this book and in the FYI section.

Phone Call Tips

1. Write a list of questions you want to ask.
2. Practice with a friend before making calls.
3. Begin by introducing yourself and briefly describing what you're working on. Then ask if this is a good time to talk.
4. Let the person know how long the call will take.
5. Follow up with a thank-you card or an email.

Complete the chart on page 32 to see how government and community groups help with hunger and homelessness. You may decide to work on your own, with a partner, or in small groups. Some spaces are already filled in to get you started.

What Government and Community Groups Are Doing About Hunger & Homelessness

Identify a Group That Is:	Key Issue	Web Sites/ Other Contact Info	What They Are Doing	How Kids Can Help
Local				
Regional				
National				
International The United Nations		www. cyberschoolbus.un.org		Student Conference on Human Rights

Taking Action

This is your tool to begin making plans for action. (If you are in a large group, work together in small groups on this task.) Start by selecting the community you want to help. Your school? Your neighborhood? The whole country? People around the globe? Then, go to Step 1.

 Step 1: Think about the needs in your community involving hunger and homelessness. Make a list.

 Step 2: Identify what you already know. Select one community need from your list:

• What is the cause?

• Who is helping?

 Step 3: Find out more.

• What else do we want to know about this community need and the ways we can help?

• How can we find out what we want to know?

 Step 4: Plan for action.

• To help our community, we will:

• To make this happen, we will take on these responsibilities:

Who	will do what	by when?	Resources needed

Service Learning Proposal

Use the information from the previous "Taking Action" chapter to develop a written proposal of your plan. You can give this proposal to others in your school or organization and to other people or groups that plan to work with you.

Student names: ....

Teacher/Adult leader: ....

School/Organization: ....

Address: ....

Phone: .... Fax: .... Email: ....

Project name: ....

Need—Why this plan is needed:

Purpose—How this plan will help:

Participation—Who will help, and what they will do:

    Students: ....

    Teachers: ....

    Other adults: ....

    Organizations or groups: ....

Outcomes—What we expect to happen as the result of our work:

How we will check outcomes—What evidence we will collect and how we will use it:

Resources—What we need to get the job done, such as supplies:

Signatures:

Project Promotion:
Finding Resources & Telling Your Story

Now that you have an action plan and a proposal, you are ready to promote your project. Write ways you can do so in each category listed below. In the Follow-Up section, decide who will do what needs to be done. If you are working in a large group, form six smaller groups and have each group focus on a category. After you come up with ideas for your category, present your suggestions.

Donations: What is needed for your project (such as flyers, T-shirts, or food)? Who might donate items?

Fund-raising ideas and resources: Be creative and invite community support.

Evidence: Chart your progress for others to see.

Media madness: Press releases, radio spots, cable access TV, Web sites—get the word out!

Presentation opportunities: Consider school and community events, like council meetings.

Partners in the community: Brainstorm all possible partners—even unusual ones.

Follow-Up

Roles and responsibilities: Who will do what?

Turn to pages 37–38, and choose a reflection activity to complete.

Make Your Action Memorable

As you put your plan into action, use this page as a scrapbook to record what happens. Add art and photos or glue in a newspaper article.

What happened today?

One page may not be enough. You may want to keep your own service learning journal in a notebook or start a large scrapbook for the entire group to use.

Any new bright ideas to help the project be even better?

Capture the moment! Add a photo or drawing of what you did or saw.

Pause, Look Back, & Reflect

Do you sometimes press the pause button on a remote control? Reflection is like that—a chance to pause and think about your experience from many angles. Sometimes the action in service learning occurs on one day, sometimes it extends over weeks or months. No matter how long your service learning lasts, these pages will help you reflect on what you've done. Write the date next to each reflection activity to help you remember the sequence you followed to pause, look back, and reflect.

Date:

What was special about today's activity? How did you make a difference?

Date:

What new things have you discovered about yourself through this experience?

Date:

Consider this quote: "If you can't make a mistake, you can't make anything," by educator Marva Collins. What mistakes have led to new ideas and improvements to your project?

Date:

Close your eyes and think about the word *hunger*. What images come to mind? Repeat with the word *homelessness*. Share your thoughts with others. Combine words with images to create a visual representation of hunger and homelessness.

Date:

Five years from now, what do you think you'll remember about this project?

Once You Know It, Show It!

You've put your plan into action and seen the results. Now it's time for demonstration—the stage where you show others what you've learned about hunger and homelessness, how you learned it, and what you've contributed to your community. This demonstration of your service learning can take any form you like: a letter, article, video, pamphlet, artistic display, performance, or PowerPoint presentation.

To help you make the most of your demonstration, answer these questions:

Who is your audience?

What do you most want to tell them about what you've learned?

What do you most want to tell them about how you provided service?

Are there any community partners who you might like to participate in the demonstration?

What form of demonstration would you like to use?

On a separate sheet of paper, write your plan for demonstration.

If you are part of a class or youth group, share your ideas for demonstration with the others you're working with. How can you best use each person's talents and skills as part of your demonstration?

What You've Learned & Accomplished

Take time to think about what you have learned, the service you provided, and the process you used—how you made everything happen. On your own, answer the following questions. Discuss your responses with the people involved in your service learning project.

Learning

What information did you learn in preparing to do service?

What skills did you develop through the activities?

How did this project help you better understand hunger and homelessness?

What did you learn about yourself?

What did you learn about working with others?

What did you learn about your community?

How will you use what you learned in this experience?

Service

What was the need met by your service project?

What contribution did you make?

How did your service affect the community?

Process

How did you help with project planning?

What decisions did you make? How did you solve problems?

What differences were there between your project proposal and what actually happened?

What ideas do you have for improving any part of your project?

What do you think is the best part about service learning? Why?

What's Next?

Congratulations! You have completed this service learning workbook on hunger and homelessness. However, this is only the beginning. You may want to find ways to stay actively involved with helping in your community. This final activity will help you determine what's next.

Write a few sentences about what you would like to see happen in your community.

What ideas in this workbook can you use to help make your community a better place?

On each step, write one thing you can do to stay involved in service.

FYI (For Your Information)

The Internet

The National Coalition for the Homeless is involved with public education, law making, and political organizing. Become super-educated about homelessness and learn the many ways you can become involved at www.nationalhomeless.org.

Share Our Strength inspires people to use their talents to raise funds and awareness for the fight against hunger and poverty. Their Great American Bake Sale program offers great opportunities to help eliminate childhood hunger in the United States. See www.strength.org.

The United Nations Web site for global teaching and learning has information on many issues including world hunger. Visit www.cyberschoolbus.un.org and click on "World Hunger" to enter Feeding Minds, Feeding Hunger—A World Without Hunger. Then click on "Youth Window."

WHY: World Hunger Year works to connect people in the battle against hunger and poverty. At their Web site, you'll find a section on Artists Against Hunger and Poverty and the benefit CD "SERVE" recorded by popular musicians. Also check out the section KIDS Can Make a Difference: www.worldhungeryear.org.

The Bookshelf

Hungry Planet: What the World Eats by Peter Menzel and Faith D'Aluiso (Ten Speed Press, 2005). This photo-journal book takes you to 24 countries to see 30 families having 600 meals. What is on their tables? Learn how poverty, conflict, and global affairs can affect who is nourished and who is not. Nonfiction, 288 pages.

A Life Like Mine: How Children Live Around the World (DK Publishing and UNICEF, 2002). Through vivid photographs, meet 18 children from around the globe and visit 180 countries. One topic explored is *survival*, which includes how we all need water and food, a home, health, and safety. Nonfiction, 128 pages.

Money Hungry by Sharon G. Flake (Jump at the Sun/Hyperion, 2001). Raspberry Hill is thirteen and knows what it's like to be homeless, and she swears she won't live on the streets again. Her endless schemes at earning money may get her some cash, but not enough to prevent her mother from packing their things, leaving the projects, and once more facing life without a home. Fiction, 188 pages.

Real Kids, Real Stories, Real Change: Courageous Actions Around the World by Garth Sundem (Free Spirit Publishing, 2010). Eleven-year-old Tilly saved lives in Thailand by warning people that a tsunami was coming. Fifteen-year-old Malika fought against segregation in her Alabama town. Ten-year-old Jean-Dominic won a battle against pesticides—and the cancer they caused in his body. Six-year-old Ryan raised over one million dollars to drill water wells in Africa. And twelve-year-old Haruka invented a new environmentally friendly way to scoop dog poop. Nonfiction, 176 pages.

A Note to Teachers, Youth Leaders, Parents, & Other Adults:
How to Use This Workbook

Young people have ideas, energy, and enthusiasm that can benefit our communities once they get involved. The question may be, where to start? By giving this book to students or to your own children, you are helping them participate successfully in service learning. The process of completing the activities helps them develop personal skills, knowledge, and abilities required to address the community needs they care about. Kids can use this workbook themselves, or adults can guide them in its use in school, youth groups, or a family setting. The following sections explain in more detail how these groups can get the most out of this workbook.

In a School Setting

This book can easily be used in various ways within a school:

Academic Class: As part of a unit of study about hunger and homelessness, whether local, national, or international, this book provides an interdisciplinary approach to examining this important issue. Students look at civic issues, analyze and compare statistics, read and discuss selections of fiction and nonfiction, develop activity plans, and put their plans into action. The series of lessons can be implemented over three to six weeks of class time when used continuously, depending on the length of the service project. Another option is to complete one to two activities per week and extend the study over a semester.

Advisory Class: Many schools have a dedicated 30- to 40-minute weekly advisory class meant to improve academic skills, provide opportunities for social-emotional development, and allow for a successful experience in a course of study or exploration. This book enables students to develop communication and research skills, teamwork, and problem solving, while working to make a significant contribution. When implemented in a weekly advisory class, all the activities could be completed in about three months.

After-School Program: These varied activities suit an after-school program. The lessons are easily implemented and include many creative opportunities for expression that vary the teaching and learning methods. Different ages of students also can collaborate successfully. Activities include partner work as well as small and large group experiences. If implemented twice a week in an after-school program, the lessons would most likely extend over three months.

Student Council: If you are looking for a way to transform a typical student council community service project into service learning, this book can be your guide. As students are exploring the issues, they can develop a project that extends into the student body. Part of the project could be an awareness campaign with the leadership students sharing with fellow students what they consider to be the most important information in this book, augmented by what they discover through research.

In Youth Groups

As service learning grows in popularity with youth groups, program staff often looks for activities that encourage academic skills in a nontraditional manner. Use of this workbook is most effective when consistent—for example, one or two times per week—so students know what to expect and what is expected of them. The activities compiled here offer opportunities for lively discussion, firsthand community experiences, creative expression (for example, writing, poetry, drama, and art), and integrated reflection.

As a Family

Family service projects provide opportunities for common exploration and experience. Rather than emphasizing the academic elements, families can use the workbook to guide them through the terrain of the service learning process while gaining collective knowledge and stimulating ideas for projects. It's helpful for family members to approach the topic of hunger and homelessness on equal ground, with the youngest members being encouraged to share their thoughts and ideas.

For every participant, this book is designed to open minds, create possibilities, and encourage the lasting benefits that occur when making a contribution of one's personal talents and skills. Each person has value in the service learning process.

Cathryn Berger Kaye, M.A.

Sources for Hunger & Homelessness Facts

Page 3: Statistics in the chapter "What Do You Know?" are from *Millennium Development Goals*, "Goal 1: Eradicate Extreme Poverty and Hunger" (World Health Organization, www.who.int/mdg/goals/goal1/en, accessed October 31, 2006); "Causes of Poverty: Poverty Facts and Stats" by Anup Shah (Global Issues, www.globalissues.org/TradeRelated/Facts.asp#fact1, accessed October 31, 2006); and *An End to World Hunger: Hope for the Future*, "The World Hunger Problem—Facts, Figures, and Statistics" (ThinkQuest Educational Foundation, http://library.thinkquest.org/C002291/high/present/stats.htm, accessed October 31, 2006).

Page 11: Statistics in the chapter "What Causes Hunger & Homelessness" are from "Famine Chronic as AIDS Devastates Continent" by Terry Leonard (*Los Angeles Times*: April 13, 2003); *Hunger in the Developing World: Many Causes* (United Nations World Food Programme, www.wfp.org/country_brief/hunger_map/map/hungermap_popup/map_popup.html, accessed October 31, 2006); and "Colombia Program Description and Activity Data Sheets" (U.S. Dept. of State: Fact Sheet—U.S. Agency for International Development: Washington, DC: July 7, 2005, www.state.gov/p/inl/rls/fs/49022.htm, accessed October 31, 2006).

Pages 14–16: Statistics in the chapter "Getting the Facts: Who Is Hungry? Who Is Homeless?" are from "Hunger in America: Who Is Hungry in America?" (The Oakland Institute, www.oaklandinstitute.org/?q=node/view/104, accessed October 31, 2006); *Household Food Security in the United States*, 2004 (U.S. Dept. of Agriculture, October 2005, www.ers.usda.gov/publications/err11/, accessed October 31, 2006); Share Our Strength (www.strength.org, accessed November 30, 2006); *Hunger Facts 2005* "HungerCount 2005" (The Canadian Association of Food Banks, Toronto, Ontario, Canada); "Hunger 1997: The Faces & Facts" (America's Second Harvest, www.nypirg.org/homeless/facts.html, accessed July 21, 2006); "Homeless Veterans: Overview of Homelessness" (U.S. Dept. of Veterans Affairs, www.va.gov/homeless/page.cfm?pg=1, accessed October 31, 2006); National Public Radio: Charlene Hunter-Gault, August 7, 2006; "DMA/WFP Report Confirms Chronic Vulnerability to Hunger in Lesotho's Poorest Regions" (Relief Web: World Food Programme: March 28, 2006, www.wfp.org, accessed October 31, 2006); "Hunger 1997: The Faces & Facts" (America's Second Harvest, www.nypirg.org/homeless/facts.html, accessed July 21, 2006); *USAID/South Africa Annual Report FY 2005* (Silver Spring, MD: USAID Development Experience Clearinghouse, June 2005, http://pdf.dec.org/pdf_docs/Pdacd880.pdf, accessed October 31, 2006); "Homeless People in Japan: Characteristics, Processes and Policy Responses" by Yusuke Kakita, 2004 (www.lit.osaka-cu.ac.jp/soc/zasshi/No.5kakita.pdf, accessed October 31, 2006); and "Unused But Still Useful: Acquiring Federal Property to Serve Homeless People" by the National Law Center on Homelessness & Poverty (Washington DC, December 2004, www.nlchp.org, accessed October 31, 2006).

Pages 19–20: Statistics in the section "When Disaster Strikes" are from "The Human Toll" by the UN Office of the Special Envoy for Tsunami Recovery (www.tsunamispecialenvoy.org/country/humantoll.asp, accessed October 31, 2006); and "By the Numbers" by the Louisiana Recovery Authority (www.lra.louisiana.gov/numbers.html, accessed October 31, 2006).

Page 26: Statistics in the sidebar "Oxfam Hunger Banquet" are from "About this Site" (Oxfam America: Hunger Banquet, www.hungerbanquet.org/page.php?id=about_vhb, accessed October 31, 2006).